BORN AGAIN

The Personal Testimonies

Of

Converted Christian Believers

by

Dr. Eddie Jernagin

BORN AGAIN

The Personal Testimonies Of Converted Christian Believers

By

Dr. Eddie Jernagin

Published By:

ABM Publications

A division of Andrew Bills Ministries Inc.
PO Box 6811, Orange, CA 92863

www.abmpublications.com

ISBN: 978-1-931820-64-6

PREFACE

Life eternal is a Supreme Idea whose origin has it rudiments in the infinite mind of God! When man whom God put in charge over His earthly creation deviated from following the Lord's Divine Guidance, death for human-kind became inevitable. Nevertheless as a result of God's Divine Compassion for his human offspring a way was instituted by the Lord, giving man another opportunity to regain the ultimate gift of eternal life!

The following passage of scripture gives credence to the loving and forgiving act of God the Father as He extends to man a second chance, and a sure way of regaining "eternal life" after such a life destroying act of man to follow the instructions of "God our heavenly father" who gave us the gift of life from the beginning of time:

"For God so loved the world, that he gave his only begotton Son, that whosoever believeth in him should not perish, but have everlasting life.

"For God sent not his Son into the world to condemn the world; but that the world through him might be saved.

"He that believeth on him is not condemned: but he that believeth not is condemned already, because he hath not believed in the name of the only begotten Son of God.

"And this is the condemnation, that light is come into the world, and men loved darkness rather than light, because their deeds were evil.

"For every one that doeth evil hateth the light, neither cometh to the light lest his deeds should be reproved.

"But he that doeth truth cometh to the light, that his deeds may be made manifest, that they are wrought in God." (KJV St. John 3:16-21)

DEDICATION

Dr. Eddie Jernagin, President of Christ is the Answer Bible Institute, of Los Angeles, California and Muncie, Indiana, dedicates this revealing book to the undergraduate students and alumni whose personal testimonies of Christian conversion have by their approval been included in the writing and publishing of **"BORN AGAIN."** May your personal testimonies of Christian conversion be an enlightening inspiration for those who may read this book and are seriously thinking of making the wise decision of accepting Jesus Christ into their lives as their personal Lord and Savior!

TABLE OF CONTENTS

INTRODUCTION

BORN AGAIN

A genuine "born again" experience rehabilitates the whole man. The most hardened criminal who yields his ways to Christ can be completely changed through the miracle of the "Spiritual birth" experience.

Society has now come into the awareness that severe physical punishment, imprisonment, reform programs, the gas chamber, the electric chair, and diverse forms of isolation do not actually reform an individual. They are puzzled as to the reason for the non-effectiveness of such programs and processes.

The reason for such non-effectiveness lies within the fact that the problems of man are deeply rooted in the human spirit. Therefore, man's spirit nature is in need of reformation. God has provided the means by which the "sinful beast" in man's nature can be changed through the spiritual process of reforming the whole soul of the man!

Only the Spirit of God working through Christ in man can balance, revive, restore, reform, and sanctify man wholly and, indeed Holy!

SPIRITUAL IGNORANCE REVEALED

"There was a man of the Pharisees, named Nicodemus, a ruler of the Jews. The same came to Jesus by night and said unto him, Rabbi we know that thou art a teacher come from God, for no man can do these miracles that thou doest, except God be with him, Jesus answered and said unto him, Verily, verily I say unto thee, except a man be born again he cannot see the kingdom of God. Nicodemus then asked Jesus the question, "How can a man be born when he is old? Can he enter the second time into his mother's womb, and be born?" (St. John 3:1-4)

Even though Nicodemus was a religious man, and an astute intellectual scholar in Jewish law, the powerful spiritual implications Jesus was trying to convey to Nicodemus concerning the *"spiritual new birth"* was beyond his intellectual comprehension. He was academically competent but spiritually blind.

There is a direct correlation between the spiritual blindness of Nicodemus and the spiritual blindness of many individuals today.

Too often there are those who feel they have been *"born again"* because they shook the preacher's hand; or because their name is on the church roll; or perhaps, because they were baptized in water as a small child. Sincere as these individuals may be, they are indeed sincerely mistaken.

AWARENESS AND CONFESSION

A genuine *"Born Again"* experience must involve a genuine awareness on the part of the person who seeks this experience that he or she is a sinner! This awareness first of all is expressed in honest confession.

"If we confess our sins he is faithful and just to forgive our sin, and to cleanse us from all unrighteousness." (1 John 1:9)

REPENT

After genuine confession is made, repentance must then follow.

"Repent ye therefore and be converted, that your sins may be blotted out..."

One must be willing to abandon and turn completely away from the things that are contrary to the will of God. The profile of the repentant person must go through a personal transition by immolating the personality of Christ.

The third step to the *"new birth"* must involve positive action on behalf of one who seeks this experience to forsake and give up his sins. The word of God tells us:

"Let the wicked forsake his way, and the unrighteous man his thoughts. And let him return unto the Lord, and he will have mercy upon him and to our God, for he will abundantly pardon." (Isaiah 55-7)

This step can be fortified each day on one's life by abiding in the whole truth of God's word. The more one lives and governs himself by God's word, the less sin will have dominion over him. The truth of God's word abiding within sets free from the bondage of sin.

"Ye shall know the truth and the truth shall set you free." (St .John 8:32)

When sin is forsaken by the repentant sinner, he no longer walks hand in hand with those things that can damn his soul. Instead, he takes on a new love which is Jesus Christ, in whom there is no sin. Thus, death, which is the inherent penalty for sin, no longer becomes his plight, but rather, he is destined for a new inheritance which is eternal life!

BELIEVE

The fourth step to the *"new birth"* experience is of vital importance.

"He that cometh to God (the Bible declares) must believe that he is God, and that he is a rewarder of them that diligently seek him." (Hebrews 11:6)

The Lord has given to every man the capacity to

believe and the Bible describes this as faith. One's faith must be released when seeking the *"regeneration experience."* Without believing that Christ died for your sins, all previous steps are nullified. But, *"if thou shalt confess with thy mouth the Lord Jesus, and shalt believe in thine heart that God hath raised him from the dead, thou shalt be saved." (Acts 16:31)*

RECEIVE

The final step to the complete transformation from death to life is that of joyously receiving Christ. If the exciting and exhilarating experience of the *"new birth"* is to become a reality in one's life, Christ must be received personally into the heart by faith. Extend to Christ your hospitality by receiving Him with thanks and praise, if you have not already done so!

"But as many as received Him, to them gave He power to become the sons of God. Even to them that believe on His name; which were born, not of blood, nor of the will of the flesh, nor of the will of man, but of God." (St. John 1:12-13)

How wonderful it is to possess and inherit the Kingdom of God within! It is a lifestyle based upon the righteousness of Christ Jesus.

****

The following expressions and Christian conversion testimonies are those of graduate and undergraduate students of Christ is the Answer Bible Institute of Los Angeles, California and Muncie, Indiana.

****

Chapter 1

WHY I GOT SAVED

(Charles Edward Kates)

I was born in August 1950 at Ball Memorial Hospital in Muncie, Indiana. My mother's name was Sylvia Lewis and my father's name was Michael Kates. They got married in 1945. They had my sister Saglenda in 1949 at Ball Memorial Hospital as well. When I was three years old, my mother and father got divorced. My mother didn't want the responsibility to taking care of my sister and me, because she was still young. She forced us to go live with my grandmother who already had seven kids, five girls and two boys.

It was fun living with my grandmother and her kids. She was a religious woman. She didn't believe in smoking, drinking, or cursing. We were forced to go to church every time the doors were open. It seemed like we were in church seven days a week, rain, sleet, or snow! At our young age we kids did not really understand what was going on in the church. We saw people dancing, jumping, screaming, and speaking in a tongue that we did not know. After church we would all go home and Grandmother would have a big dinner for us. We would get together and talk about what happened at church and imitate what the adults did.

When we became teenagers, it seemed like we were in church more than we were at home. We also began to understand what church was all about. We were in Bible study on Wednesday nights and the teacher was teaching us about the Word of God. We learned that Christ died for our sins to redeem us.

At times when we would get into mischief we would fill condemned because our beloved grandmother taught us right from wrong. As a result of our not giving our lives to the Lord we would always do more wrong than right. This would prompt our grandmother to ask me, "Why are you always getting into trouble?" I would reply to her, "Sinners do what sinners do." That was because I hadn't given my life to the Lord yet. My grandmother would ask me, "All the times you've been going to church, you have not learned anything?" I said, "No because you're forcing me to go to church." I felt like it was all a show, because all people did was sing, jump up and down, and speak in other languages that I did not understand!

Then, as time went by we all drifted apart. We had gotten older and everybody wanted to do their own thing. I had informed my grandmother that when I turned eighteen that I would be getting out of her house, because I did not want to go to church anymore. All of my friends were out partying, seeing girls, and having a good time. I wanted to be a part of that, and I became a part of that lifestyle.

I drifted away from God for a long time. During that period of time I was drinking, popping pills, writing prescriptions, breaking in people's houses, fighting, and messing with girls. Every girl I saw, I felt like I had to have her no matter what the cost. I did that for a period of time, until I was about 29 years old. During those years I had all kinds of opportunities working in factories and different jobs. Then I started to think I had better settle down and find a wife. Being with different women every night wasn't fun to me anymore. I said to myself, what better place to find a wife than in the church?

I finally decided to start back going to church. One day a young lady asked me, "what is your name"? I responded to her by saying, **"Charming Charles, the Pentecostal Playboy,"** She looked at me smiled and said, "If you want to talk to me your name is just plain old Charles." I told her, "Well we can't do business then." But I kept going to church. Then one Sunday morning, the pastor had an inspiring message. It really caught my attention, and I began to feel remorse for the wrong things that I had done in my life. I was beginning to feel guilt. At that time, I felt like the Lord was trying to get my attention.

When the pastor made an altar call I was too ashamed and scared to go. So I went out feeling sorry for myself that Sunday. But through all that week I felt like the Lord was speaking to me. The following Sunday I went back to church. We had a guest speaker there that Sunday. He prophesied to me that "God has called you and you're running away from Him. How long are you going to run?" I got frustrated with him. I got up and walked out of the service. When I walked out the Lord was speaking to me and telling me that this was the time. He said, "The time is now!"

The following Sunday I attended church services again; and once again the preacher got up again and preached another powerful message!

Again as before the spirit of the Lord spoke emphatically to me and said, "This is your last chance!" I sat there and thought about it for a minute or two. I broke out into a cold sweat! I was very nervous and scared. And even before the minister finished his message, I walked towards the front of the church and dropped to my knees at the altar. I remember as if it was just yesterday, the congregation jumping and rejoicing! The minister asked me if I wanted to be saved and I responded in the affirmative. He asked me if I was for sure, and that "this is not a play thing!" Once again I emphatically said, "Yes!" Then the minister said, "Repeat after me, Lord forgive me for my sins. I repent for all the things that I have done wrong. Forgive me for hurting you. I'm truly sorry from my heart. I want to give my life to you from this day forward I ask that your Holy Spirit would dwell in me, and that I be baptized and filled with your Holy Ghost." On that same day the pastor baptized me at the church. When I came up out of the water I was speaking in tongues and I knew that God had saved me! I have been saved ever since!

Along the way I slipped sometimes the enemy was tempting me. But all I had to do was open my heart and say, "Lord forgive me for the sins I have committed." I said, Lord, in order for me to stay saved you're going to have to send me a wife, because I am a young man and I have needs." And he reminded me *"...he who finds a wife finds a good thing."* Well, the Lord blessed me with a wife---the same young lady years earlier that asked me what was my name and I replied *"Charming Charles the Pentecostal Playboy."* That woman became my wife and gave me four beautiful children, three boys and a beautiful daughter!

TO GOD BE ALL THE GLORY AND PRAISE!!!

Chapter 2

MY SALVATION STORY

(Katrina Walker-Rollins)

There is nothing spectacular about my coming to accept Jesus Christ as my Lord and Savior. There was no drama like Paul's call on the Damascus Road. No call of God like the one that happened to Gideon as he threshed wheat by the winepress to hide it from the Midianites. No quiet voice that came to Samuel in the middle of the night, or no angel in a similitude as Paul heard a voice from heaven calling his name. Nothing spectacular!

You see, I was born to Mary and Charles Green and that meant I was "saved" from the first cry at birth. There is a saying that goes like this: "If it looks like a duck, walks like a duck, quacks like a duck, then it must be a duck." Living in my parents house meant I had to talk like I was saved, dress like I was saved which meant no pants, no short dresses, and stockings no matter what the weather was like. I had to act like I was saved and go to church all the time. But most of all, I had to look saved: Plain faced, and go to church all the time. But most of all, I had to look saved: Plain faced, no make-up, longer than normal skirts and dresses, and little Jewelry if any at all. Thank God we could press and curl our hair. The motto for home and church was from 2nd Corinthians 6:17 ***"Wherefore come out from among them and be ye separate, saith the Lord and touch not the unclean thing;***

and I will receive you." If the world was doing it, wearing it, saying it, had it, or going there, I had to leave it alone. My mother was kicked out of church just for walking through the park!

Because my parents were obedient and submissive children of God, they didn't question their leaders on the scriptures or what they did. So when the preacher taught from the Bible, they accepted what he said. If the preacher said God said it, that's what was accepted, so I grew up not questioning but also accepting what was said even though I didn't agree with what I sometimes heard or what I saw. This is partly why I think I grew up a very passive person with low self-esteem and very little self-confidence!

I was born the 4th of five children: four girls and a brother. My sisters in my opinion were very smart, talented, and very pretty. My brother was handsome and very spoiled. When I looked at myself in comparison to my sisters, I saw myself less than anything they were. I was less pretty, less talented, less smart, shorter and heavier in weight. The devil used how I saw myself as a way to entangle me in his world.

Because of the lack of self-confidence and low self-esteem, I became a people-pleaser. I would do almost anything to receive the approval of people. I did what my mother wanted me to do, what my sisters and brother wanted me to do, what my friends wanted me to do. This led to my not knowing who I was or liking myself, feeling and acting this way was a hindrance to me really seeing salvation for what it was. When you feel like no one really loves you (only tolerates you), you don't believe that God loves you either.

My life started to change when my family left the church in the Whitley community and joined Maynard Temple Church of God in Christ on the other side of town. At sixteen I started liking a boy who attended Maynard Temple Church and believe it or not, this is when I first come to see being saved in a different light. This boy was supposed to be saved so in order to go with him, I needed to be saved. Our romance didn't last very long but the good thing about it was that I didn't just look like I was saved, or simply act like I was saved, or even just talk like I was saved, I was indeed saved. At sixteen I gave my life to Jesus Christ!

I was saved on a Tuesday night and sought for the Holy Ghost on Wednesday night of the same week. I prayed, asking the Lord to let me receive the holy without having to go through all the work I saw others go through. I prayed, "Lord, keep the alter workers away from me because I can't concentrate on you with them yelling in my ears, spitting in my face, clapping their hands around my head, and having me say, same me Jesus, save me Jesus, what seemed like a million times. Jesus was so good to me! By the time the altar workers came to me, I was already speaking in tongues. Praise the Lord! God answered that prayer and has been answering my prayers ever since!

None of us are perfect, blameless, or without problems. But as I grew older, I grew in my knowledge of God. 2nd Peter 3:18 tells us to,

"Grow in grace and in the knowledge of our Lord and Savior Jesus Christ." He is a problem solver, and man did I have problems! I married a man at twenty years of age with seven children. I soon added number eight. My husband and myself, eight children, a mother-in- law and father-in-law all living in a three bedroom, one bathroom house. There were problems too numerous to mention. But God was faithful. Married, eight children (4 in diapers), working as a head start teacher, going to college, and keeping house, I was over-whelmed at times. But I learned to pray as a result of my experiences,

I never thought my mother would die. This statement wasn't wishful thinking, I really never thought she would die and when she did August 1976, my world sort of collapsed. My world changed for worse. I couldn't accept it. I didn't care about anybody, what I said, what I did or who I hurt. I was hurting and I wanted to strike back. One person told me I had changed from a human to an animal. The devil took advantage of my condition and deceived me. Earlier I said no one is perfect, blameless, or without problems. But no use in drudging up my messy past, it's under the blood. But thank God for prayer, the word of God, and great teaching that changed my life for the better. The teaching of God's word helped me to accept myself and see myself as God saw me. But, most of all, to know that God loved me. He loved me so much that he sent his only begotten son to die for me!

I wanted to honor that love and make my life count for God. But tragedy struck again. After three and a half years of marriage, my husband died of colon cancer.

This time I didn't get angry at God and go crazy. This time I held on to the God of love and the God of comfort. He brought me through that storm and prepared me for the next one, the death of my oldest son six years later. I have to give this praise report. Terry my son lived a sinner's life. He was married but had women on the side. I prayed daily for the salvation of my children but their lives were not turning around. Terry had cycle cell disease and had many crises that put him in the hospital many times. He drank, had many children, and just didn't seem to want to have anything to do with God. As he got older and sicker, I changed my prayer to God, if you save Terry and have to take him out of this world to keep him saved, I am alright with that.

One Monday night I went to a miracle service held at church. The minister told us that if we wanted something from God we needed to give him a radical praise. I had not danced in many years because of my knees but this night, I dance before the Lord and asked him to save my children. Wednesday of the same week Terry took ill and stayed alone in his room at his sister's house so I didn't go by to see him. Several minutes before 12:00 a.m., I received a telephone call from the hospital telling me that Terry was in the hospital. Thinking this was another cycle cell crisis, I told my daughter I would visit Terry the next day. A few minutes later, my daughter calls again and say's the doctors needed to talk with me. So my husband and I hurried to the hospital. As I arrived at the reception desk, my daughter comes out of the emergency room where my son was and tells me he has died. As I walked into the room, I see this light all around terry's face and his face which had severe acne look as smooth as a new born baby's skin. I leaned over him and whispered into his ear, "Terry, what about your soul, what about your soul?" I straightened up and backed away from his lifeless body and the voice of God rose up from inside me and said, "Katrina, I did just what you asked me to do, I saved his soul and brought him here to be with me." What comfort I received that night!

Had I not been saved and totally dependent on the love, mercy, and grace of God, I really think I would not be here to be reading this paper. Life has so many twists and turns. If we turn our life over to the Lord, He really does order our steps. I am in great anticipation of what else he has in store for me. God is an awesome God and he doesn't give up on us even when we try to give up on him.

I no longer have low self-esteem or lack self-confidence. I believe what God's word says about me: *"I'm the head and not the tail. I'm above and not beneath. I'm the righteousness of God in Christ Jesus. I'm a new creature in Christ Jesus. I am strong in the Lord and in the power of his might. I can do all things through Christ who strengthens me. I'm an heir of God and a joint heir with Jesus Christ. I am blessed with all spiritual blessings. I am more than a conqueror. I am a laborer together with God. I am God's workmanship, created in Christ Jesus for good works that God prepared for me to walk in. I am a faith walker and not a sight walker. I am fearfully and wonderfully made."*

In 1959 I gave my life to the Lord. There was no drama: no shining light from heaven, no voice calling my name, no Damascus road experience. But there was a loving God with outstretched hands waiting to receive me into his family. I am so glad I reached out and took His hand!

Chapter 3

THE POINT OF NO RETURN

(Brian Chambers)

It was very cold windy day and ice covered the streets and sidewalks of the bustling metropolis Cleveland, Ohio. Unfortunately, my dear mother while busy going about her daily activities, slipped and fell. Shortly after that incident I, Brian Chambers, was born on a similar winter day of January 20, 1970. From what I was told, I was two months premature and weighed only three pounds and nineteen ounces.

I believe that God had a plan for my life while even in my mother's womb. I was told that I was a very happy child and full of life (I guess I had to be after being born soon after a slip, trip and fall.) Shortly after my birth our family moved to Chicago, Illinois which was different for us because I had to get adjusted to a new even larger city and life style.

My stepfather was a city bus driver; he was good at what he did. We lived a prosperous life as children and usually had what we wanted. However, something was missing in my young life. I had no idea what it was. My mother loved us so very much! She would dress us up in our suits and take us to church every Sunday. One day while attending church services I witness her giving her life to Christ! I loved seeing her sing in the gospel choir. She was my inspiration!

One day after church I told mom that the Lord was dealing with me about getting saved. She took me in the back bedroom and we got on our knees and she led me in the sinner's prayer. At that very moment my life was changed and would never be the same again. I went on the quest to get rid of everything that was not like the Lord. My mother loved the Lord with all her heart and I was beginning to do the same!

Mother always wanted the very best for all of her children! We were transported by bus from our neighborhood to a "high academic" profile school where mostly Caucasian students attended. During the 70's that was rare in the community I lived in. The only way we could go to that school was that we had to take music. So, we joined the band and I played the trumpet, and was rather good at it, If I have to say so myself! But, those white people didn't like us at all. They threw things at us and called us names! I was trying to understand why God would have me to go through such an experience. At that particular time in my young life it was hard to be saved and be called out of my name and not be able to do anything about it. However, the Lord gave us the victory over that, and I eventually learned I had to go through some tough situations to walk with the Lord!

My dear mother had us to learn a bible verse every day before we could go outside to play. At that time in my life God had his hand on me strong! I could say something and it would come to pass!

I recall an occasion when my mother took me to a revival service on a school night across town on the city bus. That is where I would find out my true purpose as to why I was saved. The minister's name was Harlo White. I was asleep on the back pew of the church and he said, "there is a little boy on the back pew of the church asleep, bring him to me." The usher came and got me and took me to him. He said I was a special child and asked who my mother was. She stood up and said "I am." He said, "Momma, this boy is going to preach and nothing is going to stop it!" The word he will speak will be like a flame of fire that will destroy the yoke in people's lives." My beloved mother cried tears of joy on that cold night in the "windy city" of Chicago! I went home with no understanding of what had transpired that night, but my mother knew! She later explained that the Lord would use me to tell people things that I had no clue about. To God be all the glory that particular gift manifested within me today!

Later on in my young adult experience I joined the navy and never knew that the trails world get harder. A fellow navy serviceman spit in my face and I lost my religion! I beat that man up rather badly. I was detained by the MP's and was told by the physiologist that I had an uncontrollable temper.

After everything that happened, I was stripped of my rank (E4) and my pay. I went to see the Chaplin and he told me that he sees something in me that he does not see in the other young men. He told me that he sees me preaching and telling others about the goodness of God! But, I can't tell them what they are doing wrong if I am doing wrong myself! From that day forward he took me under his wing and started mentoring me and inspiring me by telling me that he could see the light of Christ in me and that's something that I already knew myself.

I knew God was not happy with me. But, I'm on a great quest now to learn the more of him. My life doesn't just belong to me and never did. I realize that "I'm no more my own but I'm bought with a price!" That price being the precious blood of Jesus Christ! I belong to him and I am, ***"AT THE POINT OF NO RETURN!"***

Chapter 4

MY SALVATION STORY

(Edward St. Claire Jernagin)

My name is Edward St. Claire Jernagin, and I am the son of Bishop Eddie Jernagin. I was born in Pasadena, California on April 9th nineteen eighty and raised in Altadena, California.

I have been attending church since I was born. Growing up I attended Sunday School, church, Sunday night services, choir rehearsal, bible study and prayer and fasting shut-in (all night) prayer services. These were all a part of my life being a pastor's son.

Most of my knowledge about God came from my parents. They always instilled Christian principles in me. Being under my dad's ministry didn't only bless me spiritually but also mentally. Inadvertently, my father has taught me how to articulate complex words. This later helped me to understand complex dialogue that I would hear politicians or lawyers use.

There were other people who contributed to me knowing the ways of Christ; Sister Artie Faye Hollins and Sister Shirley Sanders were my Sunday school teachers. At the age of five years old I accepted Jesus as my Lord and Savior, and many other times after that! I was baptized at seven, but I really didn't know what it was about until I got older. At the age of eighteen I started to stray away from God. I struggled with finding my own identity. I felt like I didn't fit into anyone's circle. I ended up making friends with people who didn't always make the best choices. They were also rebelling, as a lot of kids in high school often do.

As I have grown over the years I have learned that you cannot hide from the Lord! He is always watching you and is always forgiving, but you have to forgive yourself also. His love is unconditional and he's always there for you. I have learned that to be a Christian you should pray consistently, read your bible daily, and spread the words of Jesus to win souls! I have learned that an authentic Christian must walk by faith, be obedient to the Lord, tithe, repent, forgive, and fast at times.

I am not a perfect person none of us are; and I know that I have a lot to work on with my relationship with God, but I believe that if we do these things God will honor our works and bless us accordingly!!

Chapter 5

I ONCE WAS LOST BUT NOW I'M FOUND

(Jada' Wanna Shanne'a Brown)

My name is Jada' Wanna Shanne'a Brown. I was born June 22, 1970 to the proud parents of William Earl Brown and Patricia Brownlee. As a little girl I would always go to church with my grandmother, Helen Marie Brownlee. Every time my grandmother would get ready for church or just leaving the house to go to the store, I would ask if I could go with her. She would tell my mother or my aunts to get me ready because I am going with her. I really did enjoy going to church with my grandmother every time church doors were open even if it meant going to church and falling asleep on the back pew.

Grandmother was one of the elder others of Christ is the Answer Church in Los Angeles, California under the leadership of the late Theodore Byrd (founder) and then under Pastor Eddie Jernagin. She was very active in the church. For example she was on the mother's board, a Sunday school teacher, choir member and she worked as a nurse's aid. I have always said that when I grow up I wanted to be active in the church like she was. My grandmother died April 3, 1990. To know my grandmother is to love her! Her smile was like the sunshine! Whenever you were feeling down and out her smile would lift your spirits up. She was a precious Saint of God.

My life before I found the Lord was empty and lonely. I use to have a lot of associates I thought were my friends. Now I can honestly count on my fingers exactly how many true friends I actually have. I honestly don't recall how I felt about God before I came to Christ. However, I can say that by me going to church with my grandmother every week and watching everyone dancing and shouting all over the church, I wanted whatever it was that they had that made them rejoice and shout all over the church. I was determined not to give up until I got whatever it was that made them so jubalistic and happy!

Grandmother loved the Lord and she was my greatest inspiration until I came to know Christ for myself. She often had prayer meetings at the house with some of the older members. Every night before she would go to sleep she would kneel down on her knees by the side of the bed and pray. I would lie in her bed and listen to her. Sometimes she would pray so long that I fell asleep waiting for her to get off her knees to read the bible to me before she went to sleep. I thank the Lord for blessing me with a praying and loving grandparent. I love and deeply cherish grandmother's wise and compassionate guidance.

It was at an old fashion prayer meeting I attended with my grandmother when I made my initial decision to become a Christian and the second time it was during another visitation to church when the pastor made an altar call that I asked my grandmother if I could go to the altar. She looked at me and said yes. I went to the altar and the pastor asked me if I was saved? I told him I was not for sure. He then asked me if I wanted to be saved. I looked at grandmother for her support and she gave me a nod. I looked back at the pastor and said yes. He prayed the sinner's prayer with me. I asked the Lord to come into my life and forgive me of all my sins and make me white as snow. I felt my body shaking; chills were going up and down my body. It felt as if someone wrapped their arms around me. I started crying uncontrollably. I cried to such an extent that I felt light headed and dizzy. This was indeed an unforgettable experience!

When service was over my grandmother and I were on our way home, she asked me "How do you feel?" I told her that I felt strange all over. I feel dizzy, light headed, my eyes were burning and my head hurt. Then I asked her what must I do to keep this feeling? She told me that I needed to read my bible daily and pray when I wake up and before I go to bed at night. She also told me that, "God would never leave you nor forsake you. He knows our thoughts before we think, he knows how many strands of hair we have on our head." But, the most important thing that I remember her telling me, "I should always go to God before I make any decisions about anything." My decision was to work for Christ!

After my conversion, I noticed that I did not talk the same. Neither did I do the things that I use to do (hanging out at night and going to the strip clubs.) I stopped going to the places I use to go I no longer allied myself to the same group of so-called friends I use to hang out with that also included some Christian friends too. For example when I lost my job and didn't have any transportation. I use to hang out with a group of young ladies that I thought were my friends but it turned out that they were not my friends after all. I was no good to them anymore. When I would call and ask them if they could do something for me, they would say, "Oh I'm sorry I can't, I have to do this and I have to do that."

I went through a lot when I came to Christ. I felt as though I had lost everything but I finally realized that I didn't lose everything. I just won the love of Christ and everything that he had to offer! I don't feel the same way I did in the past. I have more of a "pep in my steps" now! God is so important to me because his Son Jesus Christ died on the cross for all my sins and rose again on the third day! He has taken 39 stripes for all sickness that we may face in our daily walk!

My life has changed dramatically since I came to know the Lord for myself. The more I read my bible the more I learn about the Lord, also learn more about the different trials and tribulations that all the people of the bible went through and I am so grateful for everything that I have in my life. I will not complain for the things that I have or don't have!

"I ONCE WAS LOST BUT NOW I'M FOUND!"

Chapter 6

"GOD KEPT ME, SO I COULDN'T LET GO"

(Nedra Lashell Rishardson-Blake)

My name is Nedra Lashell Richardson-Blake. I am 33 years old and a happy Christian! And this is my story...I am delighted to take you on a little walk with me to where it all began.

At the age of five I remember my mother taking me to church. I was sitting on the pew and the service was in session. The people were jumping up shouting and falling prostrate on the floor, crying, and making other strange emotional outbursts! It frightened me to the extent that I began crying uncontrollably! My mother had to take me out of the church sanctuary. I imagine this was a new experience for her also since we never had visited that particular church before.

As time went by we eventually ended up at New Unity Baptist Church where my entire family eventually joined. Getting up and going to church on Sunday mornings was something I loved dearly even at a young age. As I grew up I joined the pastors youth choir. It never seemed to fail no matter how much I enjoyed the worship services I was always brought to tears, even when I would sing my solos. Today, this is yet one of my emotional trademarks. As the years went on I became a very active member in my church.

I recall the day that my dear mother stopped going to church. However, I yet wanted very much to continue and she would drop me off at the church. When it was time for the altar call I went to the altar. Little did I realize that the call of God was upon my life.

When I was a teenager my father accepted Jesus Christ as his Lord and Savior, and eventually became a minister. I would go with my dad on every speaking engagement and would sing for him. One time I went with him and did not know that it would be the night God would change my life. As my daddy began to minister the anointing of the Lord began to fall over the congregation. I was standing worshiping and praising God when suddenly I heard a voice in my ear. It was a different language; the Lord then spoke to me and said for me to speak what I was hearing. As I began to obey the command of the Lord he filled me with the Holy Spirit! I was sixteen years of age at the time. From that day I knew whatever I tried to do contrary to Gods will I would not get away with it.

As I began to chronologically mature to adulthood I made various unwise decisions, but one thing I can say, I never stop going to church. In spite of the fact that I was a fornicator and a shacker! I know that some may say that they had fun living that way, but not me! I went through many years of pain and sorrow because I knew that I was destined to be set apart for the Masters use! I was filled with conviction that I was living like that and I knew in order for my life to get better I had to make some changes and make them fast! I encountered so much over the course of eleven years, but that's another whole book in itself!

My final breaking point came one night I was lying in my bed experiencing extreme depression. I was not a member of any church at the time but I often attended Greater Bethany Church in Los Angeles, California. Every Sunday I felt like something was missing. My good friend, Annie Edwards called me and we were conversing. I was telling her how I felt and she said to me; "Cookie my pastor is looking for someone to lead praise and worship. Can you come to my church and meet with him?" I agreed to do so. The following Sunday I went to Christ is the Answer Church. While there I felt this was God's way of telling me, "This is where I want you to be." In obedience I kept attending the services. I vividly recall Pastor Eddie Jernagin coming to me and sharing a word of prophesy.

The date was December 8, 1998, He told me, "Your ministry starts today." Right then I made up in my mind that I no longer wanted to do things my way. I wanted The Lord to take complete control. I always knew that I had a ministry. But it is even more convicting when the Lord sends a messenger of God your way to confirm what you already felt.

I became an active member of Christ is the Answer Church in Los Angeles, California and became the praise and worship leader and eventually the choir director. Did things in my life get better? Yes they did. February 2000 I was united in matrimony. Did I still go through trials? Some days did I feel like giving up? No I didn't, I kept telling God I trust you. The important thing that I needed to remember was that just because I said that I would serve God did not mean that problems and disappointments would stop coming my way. But what it does mean is that I needed to *"trust in the Lord with all my heart and lean not unto my own understanding but in all of my ways acknowledge him and he will direct my path." (Proverbs 3:5-8.)* Thank God he is helping me, and I will not let go!

Chapter 7

CHOSEN

(Dorothy J. Jackson

Before I accepted Christ into my life, I lived a life of corruption that was filled with sinful nature. I remember my parents always telling me and my siblings "y'all need to get saved so that you don't go to hell." When they would tell us that, I would think to myself "what is this saved thing that they keep talking about and where is the hell place?"

My parents never let us go anywhere. Although they would always tell me the right things to do, I embarked on several adventures that were leading me straight to hell! The place my parents had forbidden me to go I completely defied there wise insight.

I was the oldest of fourteen children and it was my responsibility to see that everything my daddy said to do got done! All chores had to be done even if it meant I had to do them myself because I was going to be held accountable for what wasn't done. My father was not big on accepting excuses for anything and he would hand out punishment anyway he saw fit. I had become very good at lying and looking innocent to keep from getting in trouble.

I remember my father had a tube of glue that he kept in a dresser. The drawer did not have any knobs or handles so we had to stick a nail through the knob hole to open it. I don't remember what I was looking for, but before I closed the drawer I dropped the nail in the drawer and it happened to fall right into that tube of glue. The glue started running out everywhere and I started thinking of just the right lie that needed to be told to keep me from getting one of daddy's "see fit" punishments. "Just don't say anything" I said to myself. "No one but you know who did it, so just keep your mouth shut!" Daddy came home and went straight to that drawer! "What is he looking in there for?" I remember thinking. Daddy called all of us into the room and demanded to know who put the hole in the tube of glue. I had already decided that I was not saying anything.

Daddy decided "I'll just whoop all y'all, that way I know I got the right one," How could I just stand there and let my little brothers and sisters get a whooping for what I did. Was I really going to just stand there and not say anything? Was I really going to let this happen to them? Then I thought, ABSOLUTLY! As many whooping's as I got for them not getting their work done. "This will be good for them and they owe me for all the whooping's that I've taken," is what I had convinced myself. Then daddy offered 25 cents to whomever confessed, and before I knew anything my babysitter spoke up and said "I did it daddy!" She got a whooping, but it wasn't near as bad as what I would have gotten. I told myself, "girl you did the right thing!" After that, lying seemed to get easier each time.

"GET SAVED, GET SAVED," is all my parents kept preaching about! "Why do they keep talking about getting saved and where is this hell place they are so dead set against me going!?" The only place we ever went to was church. Our church had a revival and I listened to the preacher speak. Here he was talking about the same thing my parents are always talking about. As I listened to him preach, he explained what salvation meant and how my life would change with it. He also

spoke about hell and what it would be like, and at that very moment I knew that it was some place I did not want to go. For the first time in my life I understood what getting saved really meant. So, I accepted Christ and my life has never been the same!

After I got saved I learned how to pray. Our garden was my special place that I would go to pray. I always loved people, but once I got saved I learned how to love people like Christ loved me. I became more of a giving, caring and sharing person. He chose me! He chose me as one of His and for that I am so grateful. Now that I know him, I choose to do the right thing even when it may be easier to just do wrong. Every day I crave to learn more about Him. I have a strong desire to read and understand His Word so that I may know my purpose on this earth.

I know that I was chosen by God before the foundation of the world. Because He chose me, now I choose Him. I know He is the one who will never leave me or forsake me. Growing up my parents were share croppers on a plantation called Buckskin. Our family worked hard and at the end of the year we didn't get much. However, God always blessed and took care of us. My parents saw to it that we knew about Jesus and how much He loved us. How much he loved His people. They educated us on how He gave His life for the sins of the whole world. I had wonderful parents. They didn't just talk about God, but they lived a life that was pleasing to God. My parents took us to church on a regular basis. At times, as children we didn't always want to go but we never had a choice. My parents always did what was best for us and not what was easiest for them. I remember singing the song, "Jesus loves me this I know for the Bible tells me so." This is a song that is dear to my heart even to this day. Over the years I have grown to love him more every day!

In conclusion, things have been rough at times, but the Lord has always provided a way because I was chosen! Shortly after I graduated from high school, I got married and my husband and I came to Muncie, Indiana. God provided jobs for both of us. God provided us with a way to buy a house, two cars and to start a family. We had two children, a son and a daughter. Through them, we have four beautiful grandchildren and one great-grand daughter. I truly love them all very much. God has blessed me to retire after working 46 years at Ball State University so now my grandchildren are an even bigger part of my life. Out of all the things that has happened in my life, some good and some bad, all of them are part of my process for being chosen by God. I saw them as tools of preparation for my new life in Christ. In this life I realize that without him I am nothing. However, with him all things are possible. One day I will see Him as he is. I will finally get to meet the One who made all things in my life possible.

THE GOD OF MY SALVATION!

Chapter 8

A WONDERFUL CHANGE

(Latonya Gale)

I was drowning in sin and shackled for many years! As a young girl I was raised in the church all of my youthful life. I knew of God, but refused to allow Him to be my personal savior.

As time went on I chose to experience the secular pleasures of the world instead of God. Not choosing Him as my personal savior was the biggest mistake of my life! I went through much turmoil in my life that I could have avoided, had I been saved, such as drugs, cigarettes, and alcohol at an early age and continued the habit as an adult.

My life was empty and had no real meaning. It seemed as though I could not get right with God. Figuratively speaking, I kept running into a "brick wall." Everything was falling in my life as if I was stuck in a zone with no way out. I suffered with depression and did not like being around family members or anyone else. My character reflected hatefulness as if I were a walking time bomb about to explode! I had no tolerance for anyone not even God. I carried an unbelievable weight of anguish on my head and it was hard for me to smile for being so shackled.

A dramatic change happened in my life one Sunday morning when I decided to attended church with my husband and children. Conviction began to grip my heart then I begin to feel bad because they were going to church regularly, but I refused to be a part of it. Little did I realize that a change was about to transpire as I got dress to go to church with no clue from the Lord. I was really only going to please my family.

My wonderful mother, Thomye McClellan and sister, Rosslyn Morton would always encourage me to go to church, but I would tell them emphatically no! I told them "you go to church and pray for me." My mother continued to pray the prayer of faith that she had been doing all of my life. But, my sister Rosslyn prayed and continued to be adamant and would always invite me to attend different church events, but I stubbornly refused to participate. I would ask my sister, "Why do you want me to go to church so bad? You go enough for everybody, so stop calling and inviting me to church because I'm not coming!"

As destiny would have it however, when I finally decided to go to church that Sunday morning, despite my original reason for going, God interrupted my plans. Bishop Eddie Jernagin, the pastor made an altar call and asked if anyone would like to give their heart to the Lord. I felt conviction because I knew the way of God and I was not living right. As divine destiny would have it; I found myself responding to the altar appeal and the Lords beckoning! Thank God, I repented and recited the sinner's prayer that life changing Sunday, March of 2005! Immediately after I accepted Christ I felt light, the weight of sin was finally lifted off my head!

I was tired of living in sin because it was not working in my favor. My only alternative was Jesus Christ and what a wonderful alternative it has turned out to be. After making my decision for Christ, I begin to tell others that I had accepted Christ as my Savior. Shortly after I accepted Christ I joined the Christ is the Answer Word of Life Choir that I told my sister Rosslyn that I would never join.

My life has changed for the better since I accepted Christ. I no longer use drugs, drink alcohol, or smoke cigarettes. I sing in the choir faithfully and I am now on the special pastor's praise and worship team! I attend Tuesday morning prayer services and also attend Thursday night Bible study. I have also enrolled in "Christ is the Answer Bible Institute," that is motivating and helping me stay focus in my walk with Christ.

I am very excited about Jesus and being saved and no longer suffer with depression and love being around my family and others. Now no one has to ask me to come to God's house, it is embedded in my spirit. My attitude is more pleasant and I am no longer a walking time bomb!

Chapter 9
AVERAGE GUY, AWSOME GOD

(Elder James Venable Sr.)

It's June 3rd, 1970 I've just graduated today. I'll be 18 in ten days (June 13th) and eligible for the military draft. The job I'm working on does not have a future and I don't see a future for myself. I'm just an average guy with no outstanding characteristics or abilities. I don't have a best friend or a girlfriend. There is a girl at church who I like very much and she is saved also.

I know that getting saved is very serious and that you can't get saved because of a girl. I love church and my mom and dad have taught me to respect the Lords house and His people. Any decision about getting saved should be made for the right reasons. I have thought about heaven and hell a lot, and really want to know what being a Christian really means. I see people who say that they are Christians doing and saying all kinds of things that I don't think they should do.

In the midst of all my questions about my future and church I went to a service and heard a lady missionary bring a message that caused me to get saved. I didn't have to tarry or stay on the altar for any length of time I just repented and accepted Christ into my life. I really didn't understand what it meant to be saved so I watched the Saints especially the men and tried not to sin.

I joined the choir and attended as many services as I could. I also participated in the physical upkeep of the church where my limited skills could be used. This really came into play when Pastor Jerry Maynard announced that we were going to build a new church building. He formed financial contribution teams, five members to each team. Each team member pledged to give $150.00 to the project to be given on a certain date. So, as I got more involved in the church I really felt a sense of belonging and purpose. We tore down the old building and it was a great lesson of work ethic, camaraderie, agreement and purpose. The rest of the church was preparing for the church dedication and everyone was excited about the whole thing. Our church was meeting in the basement of a former church a block away which was now a community center.

While all of this was going on I was experiencing a peace that I couldn't explain. I still had all the personal problems of a youth who was a bed wetter and who had problems expressing himself because of a speech impediment, I stuttered. All of these issues conspired against me to cause me to experience low self-esteem. And even though I was in the best of physical health of my life from playing football in high school the last two years, and playing basketball for the Boys Club, I still worried about being overweight as a kid. Nevertheless, this being saved thing helped me to navigate through my life and gave me some confidence.

Singing in the choir and leading songs was instrumental in helping me to start healing. To be out front leading songs was a great way to learn leadership skills. The byproduct of all this was that I started talking to the young lady I had my eye on in the beginning. I fell in love with her but she never returned the love that I had for her. We spent a lot of time together and remain great friends today. She was my first great love and it had a profound negative effect on me later on in my life.

It's been a year and a half since I've gotten saved and my life is rather good right now. I'm enjoying my relationship with my mother and she is proud of my involvement in the church. My dad treats me like a man and I overheard him telling a customer where we work that I was a good worker. My boss also assigns me jobs that he only trusts to a few workers. Yes, life is good!

All of this changed when I saw on television that the military war going to draft all young men with lottery numbers from one to fifty, mine was forty-nine. I joined the Air Force after deliberately backsliding because I didn't think you could live a Christian life in the military. There was also the thought that I might sample what the world has to offer.

I got hooked on drugs and cigarettes and enjoyed the life of sin that I chose. It took me about eighteen years to get myself together and realize that I needed Christ in my life. I suffered the loss of a wife and two handsome sons. I also was shot by a former friend and left to die by onlookers of the incident. Thank God that person who just drove up thought that was a pretty awful thing to do and called the police. I now have a bullet lodged on my spine as one reminder of how fleeting life can be.

Finally, after years of sinning and feeling that life had nothing more to offer me I decided to take my life. I purchased a bag of weed, a six pack of beer, and a twenty dollar rock. My plan was to get high and blow my head off with my three fifty seven magnum pistol. A funny thing happened though, I started thinking about all the things I was taught and I thought that killing myself would cause me to go to hell. So I took my gun and sold it for some more crack. I smoked it but it had lost its effect on me.

When I got to work a strong conviction came over me and I called a person who I knew was a Christian and told him I wanted to give my life to the Lord. He told me he would call his pastor even though he was an elder in his church. The pastor called and told me to meet him, his wife, and the brother I called at his church Tuesday morning, it was Monday night. As soon as he hung up Satan started working on me and I didn't show up. The spirit of conviction was still upon me and I called again and made another appointment to get saved.

I showed up early for my appointment and while sitting in my car in front of the church my drug dealer and his wife came by and circled the block and ask me what I was doing. I told him I was going to give my life to the Lord. They kind of smiled at me in a mocking kind of way and drove off. The pastor, his wife, and the brother I called showed up and lead me to the Lord. I don't remember the date back in 1970 but I do remember December 13, 1989 when I repented of my sins and giving my life to the Lord. I have learned that the key to living saved is to hide God's Word in your heart! I will never walk away from Christ again!!!

Chapter 10

THE LIFE AND TESTIMONY OF
ROBERT A. IVY

(Written in this book by Robert Ivy's Permission)

I would like to introduce myself. My name is Robert Anthony Ivy, Sr. I am the son of Pastor Kenneth and 1st Lady Missionary Annette Ivy. I was born in a small southern town of low-income coal miners that were struggling to live from day to day. That small town was called Providence, Kentucky. It was a place where one had to depend on God in order to survive life.

My father attended the largest church in town. It was a huge Methodist church within walking distance from my grandmother's house. I felt like there was no true Word of God being preached there; only vain repetitions of scriptures and community fellowship with black families being asked to support one another in their daily lives.

My great grandmother, Anna Ivy, grew up living in hard times but always trusting and depending on God for all things in her day-to-day life. She taught my father and mother to always trust in God for everything, whether it be small or great, and to know that every blessing comes from God. She taught them songs of praise; old songs with true meaning and would always sing a song to go with each message that the man of God would preach. The songs were in her and sprang forth out of her through praise and thanksgiving.

Late in the year 1951 we moved to Muncie, Indiana. God blessed my father to find work. He obtained a job as a bus boy serving rich and important men of the city at their private club. This job did not pay well, but he made friends and met businessmen who owned many of Muncie's local businesses. This was a blessing, and in the plan of God for his future. God would allow, in His timing the wonderful development for both Mom and Dad to allow Christ to enter into their lives and became born-again Christians filled with the Holy Spirit!

While searching for a church home to become a strong foundation for their lives, mom and dad were directed by my aunt, Verna Mae Pool. She was a strong black woman, raised in the South, who truly understood what depending on God meant. Hard work and struggling were a part of her life. Her church home, in Muncie, Indiana at that time was Maynard Temple Church of God in Christ. The church was under Pastor S.C. Maynard and 1st Lady Lena Maynard. They were spiritually strong, faith-filled people living and teaching the gospel to its fullest! This was the church that our family was introduced to. It became the cornerstone of our lives and drew us close in relationship to Christ.

Soon thereafter, my father received his call to the ministry and became a fervent servant of God, teaching and preaching the Word of God under the anointing of the Holy Ghost. He soon received his license and was ordained. My mother was soon to follow, becoming one of the greatest prayer warriors and teachers of the Word! She demanded that her children study the true Word of God. My mother taught us children never to leave God out of our lives. Through the teaching of my mother and other strong spiritual leaders, we were motivated to trust and depend upon God to meet all our needs. We were not only taught at home, but at church in such class as: Sunshine Band, (YPWW) Young People Willing Workers, Purity Class and, of course, never missing Sunday school class. We were even made to attend bible class in school. At that time it was part of our curriculum.

In my own personal life I had other plans. These plans did not include God but plans of natural gain. I made up my mind that I was going to leave all this teaching and preaching behind. It seemed to be too much required of a man. I thought I could make it on my own. Like the prodigal son all I could see were good times ahead. I said, "Move over world and let me pass. Here I come!" Satan's temptations seemed grand. God soon allowed me to meet a man of God that changed my life with his gospel teaching and uncompromising ministry style. His name was Deacon Myron Sawyer. His life and teaching caught my attention and there was something that drew me to him. I observed him for many years thereafter, but little did I know that one day our lives would collide and I would learn many things in life from him both naturally and spiritually.

Not many years thereafter, my father was called by God to obtain his own shepherd-ship by becoming a pastor in the Church of God in Christ. By faith he stepped out on the Word of the Lord not knowing where the Lord would plant him. Miraculously, God opened doors and unlocked ways for him to obtain a church to worship in. I was witnessing God in action. We say God will make a way out of no way, thank the Lord for Mr. Ruben Poole, my uncle, who stepped up and signed for whatever was needed financially. He put his financial security on the line. Look how God works! I was amazed how soon we were able to obtain a church facility and home rental unit located at 918 E. 1st Street, Muncie, Indiana. A church, a man, his wife and eight children; I could see no common sense in it all; especially with my father's income. Glory be to God! It was not long afterwards my father was blessed to obtain a new job working at Borg Warner. Unfortunately, I was not yet convinced that Christ was the answer. I still had dreams of leaving this scene behind in a few years.

A few years later Dad Maynard, pastor of Maynard Temple Church passed away leaving this world behind for a better place. Many of the older saints who were members under his pastoral leadership retreated to my father's church to grow in numbers and into one of the greatest spirit-filled, miracle working, God-anointed churches in Muncie, Indiana. Powerful preaching and teaching went forth by precept and example.

People began to come from all around the surrounding cities and counties such as: Muncie, Yorktown, Anderson, Modoc, and New Castle. Saints would come from Indianapolis every Sunday to worship and give the Lord praise!

Praise be to God! I never shall forget the year 1964. The church always had a New Year's revival each year to prepare the saints spiritually for the coming year. That year we invited Mother Maynard-Bracey and Dad Bracey to speak for the week. Their messages were always spirit-lead and to the point. I fell under deep conviction, and the Holy Ghost seemed to be speaking to me personally. I knew I was guilty and felt shameful for all my sins. That night I forsook all and allowed Christ to come into my life! A few days later after fasting and praying, I received God's greatest gift, the Holy Ghost! Now my life had new meaning! All the teaching I had received now came with a clearer understanding with the Holy Spirit in my life. All those years I had been running from the call of God on my life. Let me say to everyone, you can run but you can never hide from God!

First Street Church of God in Christ grew in size until we were blessed to move to a larger accommodation. I remember reading the land title abstract: "This land is never to be sold to a black man." The blessing of God surpasses all of our understanding. I thank God for it! I believe it! I receive it and enjoy it! His goodness is infinite! This church is where I grew up and was taught how to live a holy, word-filled life. After many years of training, I was ordained an Elder in the Church of God in Christ. Soon after that I was ordained Assistant Pastor. My greatest calling is being chosen and ordained by the Lord to count me worthy of the calling.

Not many days after I came to Christ, Satan tried his hardest to stop me. On my way to work one morning I had a seizure, passed out behind the wheel of my car and ran into a house at over 100mph. My vehicle bounced off the curb, turned sideways, and went air-borne, passing between several large trees in the front yard. Finally it came to rest in an old abandoned house. As the vehicle entered the house the roof of the house fell in on top of the car pinning me in the car. One leg was completely under the front seat touching the backseat, and the motor was now positioned in the front seat. I remember the steering column wheel was flat due to the impact of my body. My face was lacerated and torn from the windshield, and my body broken and beaten. A young couple found me that morning around 2:00 A.M. The police were called to come quickly to the scene as it was assumed the driver was dead from the impact. I remember the fireman saying, "Son you will be free as soon as I cut this seat from the frame." As the car was being cut away from my body, I begin to experience great pain. The pain was so severe that I could do nothing but call on God. I had no idea where I was, what had happened or who I had injured or killed. I was totally in God's hands. I felt it was my end; an untimely death at an early age. But God! Thank God for His mercy and grace! The experience taught me when the enemy says the end, God say's the beginning!

After the emergency surgery, I remember seeing the saints walking up and down in my hospital room praying and pleading the blood of Jesus over my life. Drifting in and out of my drug-induced comatose state, I saw Mother Pool, Mother Jackson, Deacon Sawyer, Evangelist Rollings, my wife, mom and dad, and many other family and friends praying for my recovery. Satan knew I was a threat to his kingdom and wanted me dead. After my operation my heart stopped beating. A code blue was called and the pain became so intense that the nurses could not remove the bed controls from my hand. They had to crawl under the bed and disconnect the control units. The surgeon had neglected to give me enough pain medication to help endure the pain after the anesthesia began to dissipate after the surgery. But God! What would I have done without Him? When I regained consciousness, I noticed all the heart monitors and breathing machinery in the room. All of the praise goes to God, I never needed them again!

Many years have passed with near death experiences of seizures and two strokes. I now know I am a living and breathing testimony of the grace, mercy and goodness of God. No one can tell me there is no God! I am enjoying my life and give all the glory to God I would not take anything in exchange for Him. I want to be Spirit-lead until the end. I can say in all honesty, "Not my will, but thy will be done." I will glorify Him until this breath leaves this old body!

This passage was given to me during my time of tribulation: *John 15:16, "Ye have not chosen me, but I have chosen you, and ordained you, that ye should go and bring forth fruit, and that your fruit should remain: that whatsoever ye shall ask of the Father in my name, he may give it to you."*

Chapter 11

LORD, YOU'VE BEEN GOOD TO ME

(Joan Lawson)

I was born in Providence, Kentucky a very small town in which the population at that time was 5,500 residents. I enjoyed being a child. I have one sister and one brother; I was the middle child.

Before receiving Christ I would fight and tell you off quick! Growing up my parents were not saved, but they were very strict, especially my mother. Even though they were not saved, my grandmother was a Christian. This being the case meant that we had to conduct our lives as though we were which also meant that we could not stay all night with our friends because their parents were not saved.

My grandmother was a praying woman. She lived next door to us and she taught us what it meant to live a holy life. We always went to church with her and we had Easter and Christmas speeches. We went to church faithfully and I loved it even though I was not a Christian.

As a teenager I would visit my aunt and uncle in Muncie, Indiana every summer. Due to the fact that they were devoted Christians one of the rules of the house was I had to go to church with them. As a result of my Christian grandmothers lifestyle I knew about being saved and I would go to the altar every summer. After realizing that I was destined for eternal hell as a sinner I asked the Lord to save me and thank God, he did!

Because I was only 17 years old, I was unsure of exactly what to do when it came to my salvation, so I stopped doing everything the saints told me was wrong. When I went back to my home town of Providence, Kentucky the people could detect there was a change in my life. One Sunday while at church the power of God overshadowed me and I ended up lying prostrate on the floor! I felt like someone was holding me down. I finally realized that this was a unique encounter with the mighty manifestation of the Holy Spirit!

I lived a Christian life in the midst of my family and friends. My life was forever changed! When I went to school, and because of the transformation that was evident in my life the teacher decided against having the traditional school party because my close friends and I were now Saints of God. Instead, the senior class took a trip to Kentucky State College. Our classmates were upset and some called us "Holy Rollers" but we didn't care, we took a stand for the Lord Jesus and today I am forever grateful for that boldness that the Lord gave me at an early age.

Because of the evident change in my life, my family had so much faith in my salvation that my mother, my sister and eventually my father accepted Christ!

In 1962, the Lord blessed me to marry a saved young man. Shortly after we married, he was called into the ministry. We have had our good times and our hard times, but God had always showed favor upon our lives. We have been in the ministry for 42 years and our only child is an evangelist.

Every day, when I wake up, I live my life to please the Lord. No matter what come or go, I still say, ***"LORD YOU'VE BEEN GOOD TO ME!"***

Chapter 12

JESUS THE LOVER OF MY SOUL

(Chester M. Tolliver)

My name is Chester M. Tolliver and I was born in Ruralville, Mississippi on May 22, 1944. My mother and father were Carry and Roger Wyett. I am one of four other siblings, two boys and three girls.

My father died when I was five years old. I don't remember too much about him, but I do remember he was a devoted fisherman. My mother was a short person with red hair. In those days they called it sandy hair. She passed away when I was only ten years old. I do remember the day she died very well. I was very afraid, when I observed what was happening to her. She told me to go and clean the house because the doctor was coming, but the physician never came, and she died that same day. After she expired my uncle took care of us for about two months. After that we went to live with my grandmother and grandfather, Roosevelt and Mary Barnes.

My dear grandmother was a wonderful and true woman of God. After my parents passed away, grandmother took all of us in. There were eight grandchildren all together and she had about five or six children of her own. We didn't always have everything we wanted to eat, but we were always well fed. Living on a plantation and share-cropping, we never came out ahead. We either came out even or in the "red." My grandparents raised chickens and pigs and that's what we had to eat most of the time. Just imagine having to share so many siblings and two grandparents with "one" chicken! By the good graces of the Lord however, we made it! Now that I look back at that experience it reminds me of Jesus when he fed the multitudes with two fishes and five loaves of bread! Even though we didn't have much, we were a happy group of individuals.

Now that I am an adult looking back on those days living on a plantation, was really a form of slavery. You worked very hard, sun up until sun down on someone else's land and they received all of the benefits!

My loving grandparents had a relationship that was like a storybook marriage. I remember my grandfather saying, "I pray to God that I die before my wife, because I don't think I could live without her." True to his word, he actually did pass away before his lovely wife. And about a week or two after his demise she also expired.

I thank the Lord for my wonderful grandparents and the values that they taught us. They always admonished us to be faithful to God and things will eventually turn out all right.

Grandmother always took us to church. At that particular time we attended a wonderful Baptist Church for about three years. We later were introduced to a "holiness church" known as the Church of God in Christ. I especially enjoyed going to this church because they were very energetic. The strict teachings stressing sanctified and holy living became an important practice in my young life and I yet hold those teachings in high esteem as I strive to practice them on a daily basis!

I was saved and filled with the Holy Spirit at the age of thirteen. I stayed true to my faith until age seventeen. However, like most teenagers, you want to experience the world and see what it is like. Unfortunately, I backslid and became pregnant with my first child. In those days they made you get married if you became pregnant. I married my child's father and it was not a stable marriage. It never is when you are forced to get married. We were together for five years and produced four children from that marriage. We eventually divorced and I moved to the state of Illinois. Later my divorced husband and I got back together in Illinois for a period of time that did not last very long.

I yet remained a backslidden Christian during this period of time. I eventually got married again and from this union one child was born. We remained married for fifteen years and finally divorced.

I later started going back to church in 1970 and came back to Christ, becoming a member of Maywood Bible Church of God in Christ under the leadership of Pastor Montgomery, an anointed servant of the Lord who taught us to live a sanctified life for the Lord. He was a no-nonsense pastor who truly loved his members and taught us to live faithful to the Lord. He also set a positive example before us and would give you the shirt off of his back. Thanks be to the Lord he did not sugar-coat the gospel of Jesus Christ!

All of my children have been raised up in the church and know of the ways of Christ. Even thou they are not all saved yet, I truly believe with all my heart that they will be saved. When I pray I believe that I receive what I ask of the Lord.

I now reside in the city of Muncie, Indiana where I am a member of Ambassadors of Christ Church where Pastor John Slaughter and his lovely wife, Dr. Ella Slaughter are our leaders, and Elder Robert Ivy, is the Associate Pastor. I love my church and all the people here, and I know they love me! I am free to worship the Lord here at Ambassadors. I am also an intercessor. We meet here at the church on Tuesdays and Thursdays, at 9am and we bombard heaven for the entire world. This is my legacy, this is what I enjoy doing. ***JESUS IS THE LOVER OF MY SOUL!***

Chapter 13

NOW IS THE TIME!!

(Dr. Eddie Jernagin D.D., D.Min)

Several years ago I was invited to an annual event as a special guest in the city of Midland, Texas. This once a year occasion was known as, the "Spiritual Explosion." My dear friend, Superintendent W.C. Kenan host this unique fellowship gathering at Faith Temple Church of God in Christ where he is the founder and Senior Pastor.

One night at this powerful gathering the keynote speaker in his preliminary remarks immediately got the undivided attention at the packed out gathering when he made his opening statement by saying the following: "Everyone seems to think that God knows everything. However, tonight I want to share with you four things that God does not know." I must admit that when he made that statement it had everyone's undivided attention including "yours truly!"

He continued his sermon by emphasizing the following points during the exhortation of his attention getting message:

"God does not know any sin that he loves!"

"God does not know any sinner that he hates!"

"God does not know any better

plan of salvation than

The one he already has!"

"God does not know any better time for you to

become a saved Christian than right now!"

If by chance you are not saved and have read the contents of this book that includes the Christian conversion experiences and testimonies of individuals who made the life changing decision to accept Christ as their Lord and savior, I pray that you will be inspired to do likewise! Please review the steps for accepting Christ as your Lord and savior in Chapter one of this book!

If you find yourself as a Christian coming short of pursuing daily sanctified perfection I pray that you will repent of your "short comings" and rededicate your life to the perfecting morals of Christian principles of holy living!

It is not Gods will for anyone to be lost eternally. Your receptivity to his gift of love to accept Jesus as your Lord and Savior will pay off with eternal dividends that will contribute to your eternity like no other gift could ever fulfill! There is indeed no better time for you to become a converted Christian than right now! You will eternally be grateful for your wise decision!

DR. EDDIE JERNAGIN

"NOW IS THE BEST TIME

FOR

CHRISTIAN CONVERSION"

WHO IS JESUS?

In Chemistry, He turned water to wine.

In biology,
He was born without the normal conception.

In physics, He disapproved the law of gravity
when he ascended into heaven.

In economics, He disapproved the law of
diminishing return by feeding 5000 men with two
fishes & five loaves of bread.

In medicine, He cured the sick and the blind
without administering a single dose of drugs.

In history, He is the beginning and the end.

In government, He said that he shall be called
Wonderful Counselor, Prince of peace.

In religion, He said no man come to the Father except through him.

So, Who is He?

"He is JESUS."

*Jesus had no servants,
yet they called Him Master.*

*He had no medicines,
yet they called Him Healer.*

He had no army, yet kings feared Him.

He committed no crime, yet they crucified Him.

He was buried in a tomb, yet He lives today.

"I FEEL HONORED TO SERVE SUCH A LEADER WHO LOVE US!"

(Author Unknown)

ABOUT THE AUTHOR

At the age of eighteen, Eddie Jernagin accepted the Divine Call to minister and over the many years his powerful and practical words have been a blessing to countless thousands!

For 37 years, Dr. Eddie Jernagin pastured the Christ is the Answer Church in Los Angeles, California. He is a noted Conference Speaker, Counselor, Bible Teacher, It's the evangelistic Bible Preaching and Teaching Ministry of Dr. Jernagin that's taking the Gospel of Jesus Christ unto the whole world.

Dr. Eddie Jernagin is a gifted writer of practical truth endeavoring to share vivid insights about life from a biblical perspective. He aspires to show how utilizing biblical principles as a guideline can provide righteous solutions for human kind to ultimately succeed beyond all negative obstacles.

Dr. Eddie Jernagin also serves as the Vice Prelate of the Governing Board and the Bishop of the Fourth Jurisdiction of The Convention of Covenanting Churches.

His messages will inspire you to search the scriptures, study the Kingdom Principles of God, mature in your faith, listen and obey The Holy Spirit and walk in the victorious life that Christ has given you.

MORE AVAILABLE BOOKS BY

DR. EDDIE JERNAGIN

Lessons For Life

Man's Inheritance

Fulfilling Your Purpose

Communicating With God

Faith Building Exhortations

Opening the Door to A New Millennium

Wise Advice and Revelation Insights

The Blessing of Tough Experiences

Devising a Christian Marketing Strategy

Influencing Your Space!!

MINISTRY CONTACT INFORMATION

Dr. Eddie Jernagin

New Dimension International Ministries

Or

Christ is the Answer

Word of Life Ministries

P.O. Box 976

MUNCIE, IN 47308

Website:

www.eddiejernagin.com

Email:

bishopeddiej@aol.com

APPENDIX STORY

KATIE

I have chosen to add this special appendix addition to the writing of this book due to the tremendous influence of my mother's life upon countless individuals who observed her as a dedicated Christian. The following discourse on her life is only a small paraphrase of her remarkable tenure.

Katie Lee (Young) Jernagin at the time of this writing is ninety seven years old! Her unique character and love for God has blessed countless individuals who have been blessed by her love and willingness to share with humanity the saving message of Jesus Christ, and the love of God Almighty!

Prior to the writing of this article I have consistently pondered the blessings of my up-bringing and all the success life has afforded me. This fortunate experience must be attributed to the love of God and my two wonderful parents

Katie and Walter Jernagin that I consider as my heroes in life! I sincerely treasure God however, above all else as the Supreme Source of all my positive accomplishments!

Katie Lee (Young) Jernagin

A most remarkable and unique woman of God by the name of Katie Lee (Young) Jernagin was born in the small southern town of Sidon, Mississippi, September 13, 1917. Katie, along with her twin brother Westly Young, were the biological off-spring of Maggie and John Young. Her father was affectionately known by the nick name of Tude. Katie also had two sisters and four other brothers who are all now deceased.

Katie's father was a successful business man who was the proud owner of three successful laundry and dry cleaning establishments located in the southern Mississippi towns of Sidon and Cougar and Morgan City, Mississippi. This was indeed quite an achievement for a black man in those Jim Crow and gross discrimination days in the South!

Katie's brother Willie and also her twin brother, Westly, were both successful entrepreneurs. Willie owned a dry cleaners in Cleveland, Ohio, and Westly, Katie's twin brother owned a night club in Greenwood, Mississippi.

Katie attended Roland Ward Elementary School. The school was located in a one room church facility known as Bell Chapel Baptist Church. Due to working in the cotton fields as a child, Katie's schooling was limited to a seventh grade education. Remarkably however, Katie who was later united in marriage to Walter B. Jernagin who was limited to a second grade education due to working in the cotton fields also as a youth. Together however, they sent both of their children Ella and Eddie to college. Both completed college and hold doctoral degrees!

Katie and Walter Jernagin were very dedicated workers who always provided for their children to have the very best regardless of their up-bringing as youth in an immensely impoverished environment! To this very day, I have never known mom and dad to have been behind in paying their bills. Their work ethics were superb!

Katie and Walter together had seven children, five of them died in their infancy. Ella and her brother Eddie are the two survivors. Both of them are now members of the clergy.

As a child Katie was taught by her mother Maggie to reverence God. Her exposure to biblical principles helped to shape her life style. To this very day at the age of ninety seven Katie, affectionately known as Mother Jernagin continues to teach others to walk in righteousness by accepting Jesus by faith as their Lord and Savior!

One of the most remarkable memories I have on mom is the relationship she had with my father who died during the month of April 2002 at the age of eighty two. Dad was a very devoted workman. I never knew him to be without a job. He was a very good loving father who had an alcohol problem that he overcame due to the devotion of my mother to God and her marriage to my father.

I often wondered in my young years of life how mom could stay with dad who had such a negative habit. She had the kind of love for dad that defied common logic! I now see that this was all made possible by her faith in God and his word that states, "For the unbelieving husband is sanctified by the wife..." (1Corinthians 7:14) Due to mom's wisdom and strength she gained from God's Word and after being patient and refusing to throw dad away, mom's prayers were finally answered after so many years of staying with dad and loving him. Her patience and love won him over and dad finally gave his heart to the Lord! He gave up drinking and smoking without ever having to go through some special man made program to get delivered. Dad became a dedicated deacon in the church and his devotion to God was parallel to that of his wife's dedication to the Lord. He never looked back and maintained his Christian dedication to God until his earthly demise.

My dear mother's love was so profound for her off-spring until after you were spanked for being naughty she would show her love by giving you some money to buy myself some candy. She would often tell me, "Son I spanked you because I love you." Needless to say at that tender youthful age I never did understand that kind of love. I look back now upon those treasured days and thank God for the chastisement because it helped to mold me into having the positive traits that I now possess today!

Mom was such a lover of children until she was appointed to be the churches children's "Sunshine Band" President. The "Sunshine Band" was an auxiliary of the church nurturing young children before there teen age years. She later was promoted to be the Purity class teacher and President. This auxiliary of the church was for the training and teaching of teenage youth! Even though mother has now retired from holding these positions, she continues to help children who are now in school with personal financial gifts towards their noble pursuits!

I am firmly convinced that the longevity of Mother Katie Jernagin, now at ninety seven vibrant years and still counting has a paramount degree to do with her spiritual diet. She daily makes it a practice of reading the Word of God and praying on a perpetual daily basis. Her life has consistently prospered because of the biblical principles she has allowed to govern her Christian lifestyle. There is life in the Word of the Lord that defies the tough challenges that inevitable confronts our human destiny. Mother Katie Jernagin's lifestyle has created a living legacy of positive attributes that reflects the character of Jesus Christ in whom she strives on a daily basis to pattern her life.

MS. Kate, as her mother affectionately use to call her has established a disciplined submission to God's call for holiness to be the characteristic life style of His human creation. This requires a daily sanctification of one's self to His holiness. By doing so on a daily basis creates a positive legacy for the world to see and strive towards doing the same by submitting to "God's Righteousness!

BORN AGAIN

www.ingramcontent.com/pod-product-compliance
Lightning Source LLC
LaVergne TN
LVHW021403080426
835508LV00020B/2431